JESUS
Name Above
All Names

JESUS

Name Above
All Names

**Releasing His Anointing
in Your Life**

JOYCE MEYER

NEW YORK   BOSTON   NASHVILLE

All Scripture quotations, unless otherwise indicated, are taken from *The Amplified Bible* (AMP). *The Amplified Bible, Old Testament.* Copyright © 1965, 1987 by The Zondervan Corporation. *The Amplified New Testament,* copyright © 1954, 1958, 1987 by The Lockman Foundation. Used by permission.

Versus marked "TLB" are taken from *The Living Bible* © 1971. Used by permission of Tyndale House Publishers, Inc., Wheaton, Illinois 60189. All rights reserved.

Some Scripture quotations are taken from the *New American Standard Bible*®, (NASB®). Copyright © The Lockman Foundation 1960, 1962, 1963, 1968, 1971, 1972, 1973, 1975, 1977, 1995. Used by permission.

Scripture quotations marked "KJV" are taken from the *King James Version* of the Bible.

Scripture quotations are italicized. Words emphasized by the author in Scripture quotations appear in italicized bold type. This emphasis does not appear in the original source of the Scripture quotation.

Warner Books Edition
Copyright © 2000 by Joyce Meyer
Life In The Word, Inc.
P.O. Box 655
Fenton, Missouri 63026
All rights reserved.

Warner Faith

Time Warner Book Group
1271 Avenue of the Americas, New York, NY 10020
Visit our Web site at www.twbookmark.com.

Warner Faith® and the Warner Faith logo are trademarks of Time Warner Book Group Inc.

Printed in the United States of America

First Warner Faith Edition: October 2002

10 9 8 7 6 5 4

ISBN: 0-446-69116-X
LCCN: 2002110843

CONTENTS

INTRODUCTION

What is in a person's name? So much more than most people realize.

A name is representative of the person; it personifies his character. It identifies him and sets him apart from everyone else.

When we call someone by his name, we are not just speaking a name. We are declaring something about him.

In the same way, when we speak the Name of Jesus, we are not just speaking a name. We are declaring a Name that embodies power — not human power, but all the power and authority of God. (Colossians 2:9,10.)

When we speak the Name, we are describing the Person. Jesus means Savior, and we are calling Him according to what He does for us — He saves us from sin, from our failures, from our mistakes and from circumstances that are not in His will. (See Matthew 1:21.)

The Bible teaches us that there is no other name which is above the Name of Jesus. It teaches us that at the mention of Jesus' Name every creature must bow, that Jesus' Name has power and authority in heaven, on earth and under the earth. (Philippians 2:9,10.)

Jesus' Name represents Jesus, so when we pray in His Name, it is just as though Jesus is the One doing the praying, the asking.

When we speak the Name of Jesus in prayer, power is immediately made available to us.

What kind of power?

Power to bless others, power that brings help for ourselves, power to enjoy the good things God has planned for our lives.

Many times in the meetings and conferences I hold, while I am ministering, I speak the Name of Jesus from the platform. When I do, I can sense His Presence and power being released in the room. I believe people are receiving healing, accepting Jesus as their Savior and becoming filled with the inner strength of the Holy Spirit in that Name.

We need more revelation about the power the Name of Jesus holds.

A few years ago I wrote a book called *The Word, the Name, the Blood.* As I was preparing recently to teach on the Name of Jesus, I reread the section in that book on the Name of Jesus. I believe the Lord was encouraging my faith in that area. I have found that God will occasionally give me a little refresher course about the power and authority in the Name.

No matter how much we may know about the power the Name of Jesus holds, there are new things we can learn, or we may need to be refreshed in things we have already learned.

The Lord does not want us to forget the foundational principles of His Word. He knows that if our faith is not stirred up in this area, no matter what we may try to do in our life, it will not work.

If you as a Christian are feeling as though things don't seem to be "working" for you the way they used to work, it may be that you have lost sight of the foundational principles in the Word about the power in the Name of Jesus.

You may think there are greater and more important things to devote your time and attention to, but you must never feel that it is unimportant to study on the Name of Jesus.

If you do not have a personal relationship with the Lord, there is something you need to know right now. There is power in His Name to change the circumstances in your life that you are struggling with. All you have to do is receive the power He has made available to you through His Name.

With His power, you should be able to handle anything that comes against you.

I would like to share with you some things I have learned about the power in the Name to enlighten and refresh your understanding.

In this book you will learn how to stir up your faith in the power of the Name to effectively use its authority in prayer.

As a minister of the Gospel, I know I need to keep my faith strong in these areas because I cannot minister without it. I must be constantly aware of the tremendous power that is released every time I speak the Name of Jesus.

I pray that by the time you finish reading this book, your faith in the Lord and in Jesus' Name will be so stirred up that you will begin to pray in a different way, that when you speak that wonderful Name, it will go forth and do what needs to be done. You will begin to experience the breakthroughs you have been waiting for in your life and in the lives of others!

God bless you as you receive this word from the Lord about the power of Jesus' Name — **the Name above all names.**

1
THERE'S POWER IN THE NAME!

❧

And [so that you can know and understand]
what is the immeasurable and unlimited and
surpassing greatness of His power in and for
us who believe. . . .

Ephesians 1:19

Imagine what it would be like to have so much power that your circumstances could not defeat you — power so great that its strength, its force cannot even be measured. In this passage, the apostle Paul tells us that is exactly what is available to us through Jesus.

Many people want to experience that kind of power in their lives, but they don't understand how to release it. An important key to releasing that power is speaking the Name in faith.

The Bible says that Jesus has a Name that is above every other Name, that it is the highest Name, the most powerful Name in heaven and in earth — and His Name has been given to us. All we have to do is believe.

What do we believe?

In John 20:31 we read, . . . *believe that Jesus is the Christ (the Anointed One), the Son of God, and that through believing and cleaving to and trusting and relying upon Him you may have life through (in) His Name [through Who He is].*

When we believe in Jesus, develop a personal relationship with Him and pray in His Name, God's power becomes accessible to us.

We receive everything God has provided for us in Jesus through faith in that Name — continual love, peace, joy, healing, prosperity, security, strength to be more than a conqueror in any situation and power to turn our circumstances around.

Think about that for a moment. When we become children of God, everything in that Name belongs to us.

Clueless and Powerless

My people are destroyed for lack of knowledge....

Hosea 4:6

Millions of people — including Christians — have no clue about the tremendous power that is found in the Name.

I know that is true because I used to be one of them.

I was a Christian for many years who went to church every week, sometimes several times a week, was on the board of my church and part of an evangelism team, whose husband was an elder in that same church. But I had no clue about the power in the Name of Jesus.

Like many, if not most, Christians today, I was powerless because I was clueless.

Oh, I "used" the Name of Jesus. I tacked it onto the end of my prayers like I had been taught. But I had no idea what I was doing. So I lived a powerless Christian life. I was powerless to bring about any real change in my life or in the lives of my family and others.

Do you know that you can live a Christian life and still live one without power? Sad to say, there are probably more Christians living **powerless** lives than there are Christians living **powerful** lives. But that is not the way God intended it to be. That was not the way it was in the beginning of the church.

The Power of the Early Church

And with great strength and ability and ***power*** *the apostles delivered their testimony to the resurrection of the Lord Jesus. . . .*

Acts 4:33

Why were there so many dynamic things happening in the early church?

Why is it that we read in the book of Acts about people being healed, demons being cast out and breakthroughs occurring in many people's lives?

Why were the early Christians able to perform so many miracles, signs and wonders?

The early Christians knew the power that was in the Name of Jesus, and they used that Name on a regular basis in the way God intended it should be used. (As we will see later, there is a way it should not be used).

When the apostle Peter used the Name to pray for a man who had been lame since birth, the man was healed. (Acts 3:1-8.)

Phillip preached to large crowds of people about the kingdom of God and the Name, and . . . *as Phillip preached it, they were baptized, both men and women* (Acts 8:12).

Paul used the Name when he commanded a demon to come out of a woman who was . . . *possessed by a spirit of divination [claiming to foretell future events. . .]* . . . . Immediately the spirit came out, and she was set free. (See Acts 16:16-18.)

It is obvious that these early disciples understood the power in the Name of Jesus, and they knew how to use that power to receive His blessings and bless others.

Power in the Name to Save

. . . stretch out Your hand to cure and to perform signs and wonders through the

*authority and **by the power of the name of Your holy Child and Servant Jesus.***

Acts 4:30

From this passage we can see there is power in the Name of Jesus for times of crisis and power to perform signs and wonders like healing the sick and casting out demons. The Word of God also reveals to us that there is power to save anyone who calls upon that Name. (Acts 2:21.)

The Bible says there is salvation in the Name of Jesus and that there is no salvation in any other name except that Name. (Acts 4:12.)

Salvation simply means believing in the Name of Jesus and making a decision to place your faith in Him. (If you have never done that before, and you would like to, there is a prayer you can pray at the end of this book).

In Colossians 2:9 we read: *For in Him the whole fullness of Deity (the Godhead) continues to dwell in bodily form [giving complete expression of the divine nature].*

Then in verse 10 we are told: *And you are in Him, made full and having come to fullness of life [in Christ you too are filled with the Godhead — Father, Son and Holy Spirit — and reach full spiritual stature]. And He is the Head of all rule and authority. . . .*

Get hold of that. All the power of God has been invested in the Name of Jesus, and that Name has been given to the church.

Wow!

His glorious Name is powerful. In order to release that power, as I discuss later in the book, faith is required. If we are seeing very little power manifested in our daily lives, we lack faith in the Name.

I can go around saying "in Jesus' Name," can pray "in Jesus' Name" and can even rebuke demons "in Jesus' Name," but if I am not really releasing faith when I pray and speak in that Name, I will not get the results I would if my faith were stirred up.

The Name As a Spiritual Weapon

For the weapons of our warfare are not physical [weapons of flesh and blood], but they are mighty before God for the overthrow and destruction of strongholds.

2 Corinthians 10:4

I believe the reason God wants to stir up powerful men and women today is because we are engaged in a war, a spiritual war . . . *against principalities, against powers, against the rulers of the darkness of this world, against spiritual wickedness in high places* (Ephesians 6:12 KJV).

This war cannot be fought in the natural, carnal world. The devil and his demons are our enemy, and we can only fight against them in the spiritual realm with spiritual weapons.

As the *King James Version* of 2 Corinthians 10:4 tells us, . . . *the weapons of our warfare are not carnal [or "natural"], but mighty through God to the pulling down of strong holds* [things that hold us in bondage]. . . .

One of the most powerful spiritual weapons God has given us to use is the Name of Jesus. (See Luke 10:17.) It is a spiritual warhead.

According to Your Faith
Be It Done to You

As Jesus passed on from there, two blind men followed Him, shouting loudly, Have pity and mercy on us, Son of David!

When He reached the house and went in, the blind men came to Him, and Jesus said to them, Do you believe that I am able to do this? They said to Him, Yes, Lord.

Then He touched their eyes, saying, ***According to your faith and trust and reliance [on the power invested in Me] be it done to you;***

And their eyes were opened. . . .

Matthew 9:27-30

I know about the power in the Name of Jesus. I have been praying and preaching in that Name for more than twenty years. But God visited me some time ago and stirred up my faith in the Name by giving me a fresh understanding of the full power and authority it holds for every believer.

Now, when I say the Lord "visited" me, I don't mean I saw an apparition. I mean He just began to deal with my heart about the Name of Jesus.

I have been mediating on Scriptures about that Name for some time. I especially do that just before I go out and minister to others. It always stirs up my faith so that when I stand in front of people I can pray for them, believing with all my heart, so that power can be released all over the auditorium to break the yoke of bondage off of people's lives.

I cannot stand on a platform and truly pray for people without really believing or having faith that something is going to happen.

When we have faith in the Name of Jesus, we can go up against any circumstance that challenges our faith with the power that is available to us in that Name.

Faith As a Force

So faith comes by hearing [what is told], and what is heard comes by the preaching [of the message that came from the lips] of Christ (the Messiah Himself).

Romans 10:17

Faith is a force. Jesus pointed out that it is a power invested, or resident, in us that can be released through prayer and the words of our mouth. (See Matthew 9:29.)

In the *King James Version* of Romans 10:17 we are told that . . . *faith cometh by hearing, and hearing by the word of God.*

If you hear the Word on healing, your faith will be stirred to receive healing. If you hear the Word on finances, your faith will be stirred up for finances.

When you hear the Word of God on the power of the Name of Jesus, your faith in the Name of Jesus will be stirred up. As you read this book, speak the Scriptures on the power of Jesus' Name aloud. By the time you finish reading this book, you will begin praying differently. You will begin having more faith in what you ask for in prayer.

You will begin to have an attitude of confidence because you believe in the power that the Bible says is yours through faith in the Name. You will be able to press on to the finish line of God's plan for your life and enjoy all the blessings that He has set aside for you! You will have stirred up your faith in the power of the glorious Name of Jesus — **the Name above all names.**

2

THE NAME AND FAITH

~

For all the promises of God in Him are Yes,
and in Him Amen, to the glory of God
through us.

2 Corinthians 1:20 NKJV

There are many promises in the Bible
that we read but never see come to pass
in our life.

Why is that? What is the problem?

First of all, we must realize that all
privileges are released through believing,
not simply because they are written in
the Bible.

~

They are not even released to us just because we believe in Jesus. They are released to us because we believe the promises are true, and we put our faith in those things that God has said.

As we have seen, in Ephesians 1:19 the apostle Paul wrote, *And [so that you can know and understand] what is the immeasurable and unlimited and sur-passing greatness of His power in and for us who believe. . . .*

I don't believe he was just saying, "I want you to know the immeasurable power that is available to those of us who believe in Jesus." I believe he was saying, "I want you to know the immeasurable power that is available to those of us who believe in Jesus — **and who believe that power is ours."**

We sometimes think that just because we have general faith in Jesus as Lord and Savior, everything promised us in the Bible will come to pass in our life as a matter of course.

That is not the way faith works. We have to appropriate the specific promises through faith.

Let me give you an example from the Word of God.

Signs Follow Those Who Believe

And these signs shall follow them that believe;
In my name shall they cast out devils; they
shall speak with new tongues;

*They shall take up serpents; and if they
drink any deadly thing, it shall not hurt
them; they shall lay hands on the sick, and
they shall recover.*

Mark 16:17,18 KJV

These promises were given to the disciples just after Jesus conferred power and authority upon them and just before He ascended into heaven to sit at the right hand of the Father. (v. 19.)

I don't believe all these things happen just to those who believe in Jesus. I believe that supernatural signs follow those **who believe in Jesus and believe the signs are going to follow them.**

The church of Jesus Christ is full of unbelieving believers. I know because, as I said earlier, I was a Christian for many years. I was born again. If I had died, I would have gone to heaven, but I lived a totally powerless life.

I believed in Jesus Christ, but I did not believe in the power of His Name because nobody had ever taught me about that power. I had never heard anybody preach about it. I thought God was the only One Who had any power, and if He chose to use it in my life, He would do so. If He didn't choose to use it in my life, there was nothing I could do about it.

I knew nothing about the power of praying in the Name of Jesus. Although I tacked "in the Name of Jesus" onto the end of my prayers, I didn't know what I was doing.

When I was baptized in the Holy Spirit and began to learn about the authority of the believer, I started believing I had power.

We become baptized in the Holy Spirit (receive divine power to accomplish His will in our life) the same way we become saved. We pray, asking God.

When we as believers in Jesus Christ are baptized in the Holy Spirit, the Holy Spirit enables us to receive, understand and experience the power of God in a greater way.

When I started believing I had the power of God available to me, I started using it by praying in the Name of Jesus. When I started using it, I started seeing powerful things happen in my life and in the lives of those around me.

It is not enough just to believe in Jesus. We have got to believe in the power of His Name — and the fact that we have that power.

Do you believe and confess that you are weak or that you are powerful?

If we have that immeasurable power available to us, we don't really realize it if we respond to circumstances by saying things like: "I just can't take any more of this — I'm beaten"; "I can't go on like this anymore — it's too much for me"; "I feel like I'm falling apart — everything's crashing down on my head. This is too hard for me. I can't stand it. I can't . . . I can't . . . I can't. . . ."

The problem is that we don't really believe we have the power. We may talk about the power and sing about it, but in reality we believe what we feel more than what the Bible says.

Sometimes we make our feelings our god.

So perhaps the reason the signs are not following us is that we don't **believe** they will follow us.

Just Believe!

And Jesus said, [You say to Me], If You can do anything? [Why,] all things can be (are possible) to him who believes!

Mark 9:23

Every time I stand in front of a group of people to minister to them, I believe that I am being led by the Holy Spirit[1] and that He will minister to the people by

38

working through me to meet their needs. (See 1 Corinthians 12:4-11.)

When I step out onto that platform, I know what I am going to preach, but I don't know anything about the rest of the service. I don't have a clue about what is going to take place. I just believe that signs are going to follow me because the Bible says so. (See Mark 16:17,18.) I believe God is leading me by His Spirit.

As a result (and I don't say this haughtily or in pride), we don't have bad services. It just doesn't happen. We go home after every meeting shaking our heads, saying, "God just blew us away! He is so-o-o good!"

The power of God can be felt so strongly in the services. The anointing seems to build and build in every session. There have been times that we have seen as many as thirteen hundred people baptized in the Holy Spirit in one service. People are always healed physically and emotionally as well as spiritually.

And it all happens because we **believe** — because we put faith in the Name of Jesus and in Who He is. It is *all* because of Jesus — His goodness, His mercy and the power in His wonderful Name.

Look At Jesus

And His name, through and by faith in His name, has made this man whom you see and recognize well and strong. . . .

Acts 3:16

If we want to enjoy the power in the Name, we cannot look at ourselves and at everything we are **not.** We must look at Jesus and at everything He **is** and is willing to do for us and through us.

In my ministry I encourage the members of our worship team to believe that when they begin to lead praise and worship, demons are going to have to flee and people are going to be saved, healed and filled with the Holy Spirit.

In my conferences I don't do anything to waste time or to impress anyone. I am there for one reason, and that is to set captives free. If I didn't really believe that what I am doing is helping people, I would stay home with my children and grandchildren.

But I do believe with all my heart that what I am doing is meeting the needs of thousands of people. I believe that when I pray in the Name of Jesus, things are going to happen — and they do!

I am not just doing it to be doing it. I believe it is working and changing lives!

If your life is in a mess, if you are not winning against your circumstances, then check your believing.

Remember, Jesus Himself said: . . . *According to your faith . . . be it done to you* (Matthew 9:29).

Pray and Believe

. . . whatever you ask for in prayer, believe (trust and be confident) that it is granted to you, and you will [get it].

Mark 11:24

You may say, "Well, I pray in the Name of Jesus, and I still don't get any results."

You may be praying in the Name of Jesus at one time of the day, but without realizing it, using the Name frivolously the rest of the day. Or it may be that you are praying in the Name of Jesus, but you are tacking it on to the end of your prayers like a little magic charm!

If so, from now on when you speak the Name of Jesus, speak it in faith, believing that limitless power is being made available to you.

When I do that, I can feel the power in that Name. I can feel it going through me.

The Bible is not joking when it says that there is power in that Name.

When I speak the Name of Jesus on television, I believe that power goes through the airwaves and right into people's homes to meet the needs of all those who hear it and receive it in their heart by faith.

There is salvation in the Name of Jesus. There is healing in that Name and deliverance from depression and oppression. There is breakthrough in that Name.

To receive everything that is in the Name, all you have to do is sincerely believe.

The Name and the Word

If you live in Me [abide vitally united to Me] and My words remain in you and continue to live in your hearts, ask whatever you will, and it shall be done for you.

John 15:7

I think that sometimes we Christians lift that promise from Jesus out of context. We think we can ask for anything **we** want, and the Lord has to give it to us because we tack His Name onto the end of our prayers.

The way to interpret Scripture is to interpret it in the light of other Scripture. We can't just pull John 15:7 out of context without considering 1 John 5:14,15 which says in essence that if we ask anything according to **His** will, He will grant our request.

In the *King James Version* of John 15:7 the Lord says, *If ye **abide** in me, and my words **abide** in you, ye shall ask what ye will, and it shall be done unto you.*

I used to think that was the most awesome Scripture I had ever read. The word *abide* means "To rest, or dwell. . . . To continue permanently. . . . to be firm and immovable."[2] By the time I finally began abiding in Jesus, I had learned that my will had become one with His will so that I really didn't want anything that was not the will of the Lord.

To this day, if I have a Scripture to back up what I am asking for in prayer, I will go before the Lord and say, "This is Your Word, and I am expecting it to be fulfilled in my life."

But there are many things we pray about for which we do not have a specific Scripture. In those cases, we have to pray, "Lord, this is what I believe I want in this situation. If it is right, I trust You will give it to me; but if it is not right, then I don't want it, because I only want Your will."

Not My Will, but Your Will

And He withdrew from them about a stone's throw and knelt down and prayed,

Saying, Father, if You are willing, remove this cup from Me; yet not My will, but [always] Yours be done.

Luke 22:41,42

My younger son was nineteen years old when he got married. We knew he was young, but we were all for it. The girl he married was only eighteen, but she came from a minister's family and had a strong relationship with the Lord. They were as cute as they could be.

47

They received some money as part of their wedding presents, and they had some more from their savings, so they had enough to make a down payment on a little house, if it was not too expensive.

My husband had taught our son a lot of good principles about how to handle money. He didn't want to throw his money away paying rent if he could buy a house of his own.

So we went with them to look for a house. They found one that they liked and could afford. They were really excited about it.

The next day our son told us, "Charity and I went out last night and sat in front of that house and prayed, 'Lord, if it is Your will for us to have this house, then we want it. If it is not Your will for us to have it, then we know You have something better for us. We only want what is Your will.'"

As it turned out, before they could get back to buy the house, someone else bought it.

"We were disappointed," he told us later. "But I just believe that house sold because God has something better for us, and we are just going to wait for it."

That is the way we need to pray when we are not sure that what we are asking for is God's will for us based on His Word.

It would not have been wise for our son and his bride to have gone out and sat in front of that house and prayed, "In the Name of Jesus, this house is ours, and we are not going to have any other house! Father, this is the house we want, and we believe You are going to get it for us because Jesus said we can have whatever we ask for in His Name!"

We can have whatever we ask for in prayer, **if** we know that what we are asking is the will of God for us — and not just our own will.

We find God's will for us by praying and by reading His Word. Then when we apply our faith according to His Word for our life, we can claim what is rightfully ours and use the Name of Jesus with results.

3

USING THE NAME

*And it shall be that whoever shall call upon
the name of the Lord [invoking, adoring, and
worshiping the Lord — Christ] shall be saved.*

Acts 2:21

A friend of mine, whom I taught in
Bible college and who went on to pastor
a church, gives a vivid example of calling
on the Name in a crisis.

One day when he had his little son who
was about three or four years old in the
car with him, he was driving through a
busy intersection and preparing to make
a right-hand turn. He did not know that

the boy's door was not locked. When he began to make the right turn, their weight was thrown to that side of the car. This happened before seat belt laws were passed, and the child was not wearing one.

When the man made that sharp turn, the car door flew open, and the little boy rolled out of the vehicle right into the middle of the intersection and into oncoming traffic!

The father remembered seeing traffic coming from all four directions and was horrified as he saw a set of car wheels moving at a very fast rate of speed — just about to roll on top of his son. The only thing he could do was cry, "JESUS!"

The father stopped his car, jumped out and ran to his little boy, who was perfectly all right. Then he turned to the man who had almost run over his son and cried, "Thank you, thank you, thank you for stopping your car in time!"

But the man driving the car that had almost hit the child was absolutely hysterical. My friend went over to him and started trying to comfort him.

"Don't be upset!" he said. "My son is all right — he's OK. Don't be concerned about it. Just thank God you were able to stop!"

The man was shaking as he said repeatedly, "You don't understand! You don't understand!"

"What's wrong?" the father asked.

"I never even put my foot on the brake!" the man responded.

The power in the Name stopped that car! This was a crisis situation. There was no time for anyone to do anything — no time to think, plan or reason. Although there was nothing the man could do, the Name of Jesus prevailed. Because miracle-working power came on the scene, the boy's life was spared.

Power and Authority in the Name

Then Jesus called together the Twelve [apostles] and gave them power and authority over all demons, and to cure diseases,

And He sent them out to announce and preach the kingdom of God and to bring healing.

Luke 9:1,2

In my meetings we always have a time of ministry in addition to the preaching.

I used to have prayer lines in which I prayed for people individually. I love to do that, but my meetings have grown, and if I did that, I wouldn't get anything else done.

I have learned that I can stand and pray in the Name of Jesus, releasing my faith, and people in the congregation can receive that healing power just as surely as if I prayed with each one of them individually.

When people come into my meetings burdened and depressed, I have learned to take authority over those spirits in the Name of Jesus so that heaviness is lifted, and the people are able to leave in freedom and joy.

But it is not my prayer that breaks those yokes of bondage; it is the power and authority in the Name of Jesus that does it. My prayer is simply the vehicle that carries the power.

The Power of Attorney

. . . All authority (all power of rule) in heaven and on earth has been given to Me.

Go then and make disciples of all the nations, baptizing them into the name of the Father and of the Son and of the Holy Spirit,

Teaching them to observe everything that I have commanded you, and behold, I am with you all the days (perpetually, uniformly, and on every occasion), to the [very] close and consummation of the age. Amen (so let it be.)

Matthew 28:18-20

In this passage, Jesus is essentially saying, "All power and authority in heaven and on earth have been given to Me, and now I am giving it to you. Go and do the works that I have done, and even greater works than these shall you do — in My Name." (John 14:12.)

In other words, Jesus has given all who believe in Him the power of attorney or the legal right to use His Name.

There is no reason for us to be whiny, wimpy, weak or powerless. There is no reason for us to ever give up and quit. We will feel like quitting if we have not been using the Name of the Lord to the degree that it is available to us because we will have no victory and will find ourselves struggling all the time. We must avoid using the Name to make frivolous statements like, "Oh, my God, I'm so hot"; "I'm so cold"; "I'm so tired"; "My God, I'm so hungry"; "I'm so weak."

When we speak that glorious Name, we need to speak it purposely with reverence and respect, recognizing the power and authority that it contains.

We need to know that when we speak Jesus' Name, we are calling forth into our atmosphere everything that He is. His Name represents Him. It takes His place. When His Name is spoken, He is there.

That's what it means to have power of attorney.

I have power of attorney over the affairs of my aunt. I am authorized to sign her checks, spend her money, pay her bills or sell her property. I have that power and authority because she gave it to me in the form of power of attorney.

That is what Jesus has done for you and me. He has given us the right to speak to circumstances, principalities and powers with the authority bestowed on us by the power of attorney He invested in us. We exercise that power of attorney by using His Name.

The Name Gets Attention!

... He Himself became as much superior to angels as the glorious Name (title) which He has inherited is different from and more excellent than theirs.

Hebrews 1:4

According to the Bible, when the Name of Jesus is spoken, all heaven pays attention.

I wouldn't be a bit surprised if, when we sincerely and reverently and faithfully speak the Name of Jesus, all of heaven says, "Shhhhhh."

Why do we all like to know somebody important? Because we like to be name-droppers. We like to use that person's name because it gives us an added measure of importance.

My daughters have learned that is true.

At my office I can't take every call that comes in or I would never get any work done. So when people try to call me there, they usually have to speak to one of my assistants or leave a message on my voice mail. The same is true for most of my managers. It's hard to get through to them personally because they are so busy.

Sometimes when I am at home, I will say to one of my daughters, "Call Roxane [my general manager] and get her on the phone for me because I need to talk to her."

Now my children are important, and they are respected at the ministry, but they know their names don't get nearly as much attention as mine.

So if my daughter Sandra calls the ministry and says, "This is Sandra, and I need to talk to Roxane," she won't have nearly the same results as if she calls and says, "I'm calling for my mother, and I need to talk to Roxane."

I have told my staff that when I call in, they need to put my calls straight through because I may be out on the road and not have time to wait or another chance to call back.

So my daughters have learned if they will use my name, it will get them more attention and quicker results.

That is the way we ought to be with the Name of the Lord. We need to be "Name-dropping" the right Name — the Name of Jesus. We need to make sure we are using it to get the attention and the results we require in order to receive all God has for us and do all He wants us to do.

Using the Name in Prayer

I assure you, most solemnly I tell you, if anyone steadfastly believes in Me, he will himself be able to do the things that I do; and

he will do even greater things than these,
because I go to the Father.

And I will do [I Myself will grant] whatever
you ask in My Name [as presenting all that I
AM], so that the Father may be glorified and
extolled in (through) the Son.

[Yes] I will grant [I Myself will do for you]
whatever you shall ask in My Name [as
presenting all that I AM].

John 14:12-14

I don't mean to sound super-spiritual, but when I pray, I like to say the Name of Jesus in a certain way — rather deliberately with some special emphasis. Probably 75 percent of my prayer time is spent in praise and worship. I have found that thanksgiving needs to outweigh petition.

It is fine to ask God for what we want. Jesus told us to ask in His Name. But if we are praisers and worshippers, if we are thankful and grateful, we can spend the majority of our prayer time praising and worshipping the Lord. Then we can mention our need in the Name of Jesus, and He will move quickly to meet our need.

Many times in my personal prayer time, which is very important to me, I will enter into the presence of the Lord and just speak that Name over and over: **Jesus, Jesus, Jesus. I love You, Jesus. I magnify Your Name. I lift up Your holy Name.**

I have learned that when I speak that Name, power is released to set the captives free and to break bondages off people.

When I speak it, I expect the sick to be healed and demons to be cast out.

That power and authority is not given just to me. The power in that Name is available to every believer.

You never know what may happen if you as a believer lay your anointed hand on someone and say, "Be healed, in Jesus' Name."

Many times when we sing songs about the Name of Jesus, we don't really understand the message the Lord is trying to give us. In *The Amplified Bible* version of John 14:12-14 Jesus says that when we pray in His Name, we are presenting to the Father all that Jesus is.

I like that because it takes the pressure off of me. I am not presenting what I am or have been or hope to be, because I make mistakes and do things wrong.

When I pray, **Father, I come to you in Jesus' Name; by faith I put the blood of Jesus over my life;[1] I ask You to forgive me for all my sins,[2] and I come in that Name that is above every other Name,** I am presenting to the Father all that His Son Jesus is. I am reminding Him of the sacrifice that He made for me when . . . *He came once for all . . . to put away the power of sin forever by dying for us* (Hebrews 9:26 TLB) on the cross and then rising again on the third day. I am declaring my faith in Jesus, so that my sins are not even in the picture anymore.

When I minister in a meeting, I expect to see powerful things come to pass. I am not trying to glorify my name or build my reputation.

My job is simply to stand up and speak the Name. My job is to pray for the people, and leave the results to the Lord. I want His Name to be glorified and lifted up. I want people to know there is power in the Name of Jesus.

Pray Your Way through Your Day

*Now Peter and John were going up to the temple **at the hour of prayer,** the ninth hour (three o'clock in the afternoon),*

[When] a certain man crippled from his birth was being carried along,

who was laid each day at that gate of the temple [which is] called Beautiful, so that he

67

might beg for charitable gifts from those who entered the temple.

So when he saw Peter and John about to go into the temple, he asked them to give him a gift.

And Peter directed his gaze intently at him, and so did John, and said, Look at us!

And [the man] paid attention to them, expecting that he was going to get something from them.

But Peter said, Silver and gold (money) I do not have; but what I do have, that I give to you: **in [the use of] the name of Jesus Christ of Nazareth,** *walk!*

Acts 3:1-6

If we would pray more for people in the Name of Jesus instead of judging them, we would see more breakthroughs in their lives and in ours. After all, it takes less time to pray than it does to judge and criticize.

Let me give you an example.

Suppose we see a young man walking down the street. Because he is stumbling, we assume he must be stoned on drugs or drunk on alcohol. Since he is dirty and unkempt, we figure he is probably homeless.

How many times do we look at such a person and say to ourselves, "What a shame for anybody to waste their life like that. What a terrible way to live. I just can't believe people let themselves get into such a sorry state."

69

Yet it would take much less time and energy to simply say, "Father, in Jesus' Name I pray for that young man to be delivered from his distressing situation. Send the perfect laborer into his path, someone he will listen to, someone who can speak a word in season to him. Thank You, Lord, that from this moment forward You are going to work in his life so that he will no longer be lost."

Like Peter and John in the passage in Acts 3, we need to learn to pray our way through the day and rid ourselves of the mentality that prayer is a physical posture we assume somewhere at home or in church. Thinking that we need to be eloquent or sound fancy before God will hear our prayer is a mindset we need to overcome.

Prayer is simply talking to God. And we can do that every day, all day long. Like Peter and John, we need to pray in the Name of Jesus — with faith in that Name. Praying in the Name is part of our inheritance rights (as sons and daughters of God) through the blood of Jesus.

There is power in the blood of Jesus, just as there is power in the Name of Jesus.

There Is Power in the Blood

For if [the mere] sprinkling of unholy and defiled persons with blood of goats and bulls and with the ashes of a burnt heifer is sufficient for the purification of the body,

*How much more surely shall the blood of
Christ, Who by virtue of [His] eternal Spirit
[His own preexistent divine personality] has
offered Himself as an unblemished sacrifice to
God, purify our consciences from dead works
and lifeless observances to serve the [ever]
living God?*

Hebrews 9:13,14

I love to talk and sing about the Name
of Jesus and about the blood of Jesus
because I firmly believe that when we do,
if we are sincere, demons have to flee.

If you want to create an atmosphere for
miracles, just start praying, singing,
preaching and exhorting about the
Name and the blood of Jesus.

**There is power in the blood, enough
power to wash away a lifetime of sin.**

Think about what you and I have. We have the Name and the blood of Jesus. The blood completely cleanses us from all our sins so that we are made as clean as if we had never sinned at all. (1 John 1:7.) All the power of heaven and earth is invested in the Name of Jesus, and that Name is given to us.

Now that we are washed in the blood, we can go forth, confident that whatever we ask or speak, Jesus has promised to provide and fulfill because we speak in the power of His Name, as presenting all that He is.

Don't put up with living a powerless life. Learn to use the power of God that

is available to you by using the Name in
prayer and praise — not in vain.

4

TAKING THE NAME IN VAIN

~

Thou shalt not take the name of the Lord thy God in vain; for the Lord will not hold him guiltless that taketh his name in vain.

Exodus 20:7 KJV

The Amplified Bible version of this verse reads: *You shall not use or repeat the name of the Lord your God in vain [that is, lightly or frivolously, in false topic affirmations or profanely]; for the Lord will not hold him guiltless who takes His name in vain.*

Several years ago I received a revelation about this subject of taking the Name of the Lord in vain.

Up to that time I had always thought taking the Name of the Lord in vain amounted to tacking His Name onto a curse word, or using it in some other form of profanity.

But when I read this verse which speaks about using His Name *lightly or frivolously,* the Lord began to show me how many times we believers — not just unbelievers — misuse His Name.

We use the word "God" in so many ways, and many times we are no more seriously praying or calling upon the power in that Name than on the man in the moon. We are just casually throwing it around. That is taking the Name of the Lord in vain just as much as using it profanely.

Mixing Positives and Negatives

Does a fountain send forth [simultaneously] from the same opening fresh water and bitter?

James 3:11

I believe one of the reasons we are not seeing power released in the Name of the Lord is that in our speech we are mixing positives and negatives. When we do that, we come up with zero.

When we need a breakthrough, we cannot use the Name of the Lord positively, then turn right around and use it negatively and still expect it to have power.

The Lord spoke to me about that very situation (not in an audible voice, but in my spirit). He said, "Some people never get anywhere because they are positive one day and negative the next day about the same thing."

When we pray and make a good confession in line with the Word, the angels go to work on our behalf. (See Psalm 103:20 and Hebrews 1:14.) But when we become weary and begin to grow faint in our mind and start saying all kinds of negative things, we start undoing everything we have been praying about. We end up right back where we started.

When people say something like, "Oh, my God — I'm so tired," they are not praying. They are not talking to God.

They are just using a phrase to express their feelings.

Now it's fine to say, "Oh, my God — I'm so tired," when we are truly lifting up our heart to the Lord in earnest prayer about being in that condition. But most of the time this is not what we are doing. Without thinking about it, we are using the Name of the Lord in a light or frivolous manner. As we have seen, God has made it clear in His Word that anyone who does that will not be held guiltless. That is why we need to be careful about how we use that Name.

Everywhere I go I hear people, even believers, saying things like, "Oh, Lord," or, "Dear God," when they are not addressing Him at all. Using the Lord's

Name in that way has become a habit. They have a habit of making statements such as:

"My God, grocery prices are high these days."

"Lord, it's hot in here."

"Dear God, I'm cold."

"Good Lord — I'm so hungry I think I'm going to die."

I hear such language even when I am with preachers, intercessors, worship leaders or missionaries, etc. In fact, I hear it so often that there is no point in trying to correct them every time they do it. But it grieves me because I know they are hurting themselves severely when they do that.

The Lord has shown me that many people in the body of Christ need to improve dramatically in this area. We all need more reverence for the Name.

Reverence for the Name

*... let us have grace, whereby we may serve God acceptably **with reverence** and godly fear.*

Hebrews 12:28 KJV

I will not sit and watch television programs or movies in which the Name of the Lord is taken in vain. It doesn't matter what the show is about or how much my family and I may want to see it, if it takes the Name of the Lord in vain — off it goes.

Why?

Because that is irreverence. I love the Lord too much to be entertained by someone taking His Name in vain. He has done too much for me to do that.

I truly believe that if we expect the Name of the Lord to release power in our life when we need it, then we must reverence that Name the rest of the time.

Most of us today have no idea what reverence the people had for the Name of the Lord under the Old Covenant. They had such awe for it that they wouldn't even speak it. Many times they just referred to it as "that Name" because they knew the power that was in the Name.[1]

David lived under the Old Covenant when he faced Goliath, the giant champion of the Philistines (Israel's enemy)

who cursed David by his gods and threatened to give his . . . *flesh to the birds of the air and the beasts of the field* (1 Samuel 17:43,44).

David was in a crisis situation, but he answered the enemy's threats by declaring, *. . . You come to me with a sword, a spear, and a javelin, but I come to you in the name of the Lord of hosts, the God of the ranks of Israel, Whom you have defied* (v. 45).

Then David said, "I'll have your head today!" (v. 46).

When David went out to do battle against that heavily armed giant, he carried with him nothing but a slingshot and the Name of the Lord. But that was more than enough to defeat his brazen enemy.

That's what you and I need to do when we encounter opposition from our spiritual enemy, the devil. We need to use the spiritual weapons the Lord has provided for us, and, as we have already seen, one of those weapons is the Name. The Name of Jesus pierces the darkness.

Deal with the Spirit
Behind the Problem

For we are not wrestling with flesh and blood
[contending only with physical opponents],
but against the despotisms, against the powers,
against [the master spirits who are] the world
rulers of this present darkness, against the
spirit forces of wickedness in the heavenly
(supernatural) sphere.

Ephesians 6:12

When someone is aggravating or frustrating us, it doesn't do any good to judge or criticize that individual. In the Name of the Lord we need to deal with the spirit that is behind that person.

There have been times, like on the golf course, when I have been around people who just constantly curse. In those times I have learned to get away by myself and say, "In Jesus' Name I take authority over you, vile demon of cursing. You shut your mouth. I am not going to listen to that all day."

At others times I hear people criticizing, murmuring, grumbling and faultfinding — and I am supposed to spend the whole day with them! Again, I get away somewhere and say, "Father, I take authority over that critical spirit and bind it in Jesus' Name. I am not going to listen to that all day long." (See Matthew 18:18.)

Sometimes people ask me, "Do you always get instant results?"

The answer is no. People have a free will, and they can override my prayer and confession. But I am learning in my own life to pray first before taking any other action. Prayer is a positive, energizing way to handle problems. If I need to say something directly to the individual, I will, but I always want to follow the Holy Spirit's leading in these types of situations.

The point is, we need to be more prayer-ful about the people and situations we come in contact with every day. We need to remember that there is power in the Name of Jesus.

The Name Is No Joke!

Let there be no . . . foolish and sinful (silly and corrupt) talk . . .; but instead voice your thankfulness [to God].

Ephesians 5:4

Another thing I got into the habit of doing that God really chastised me about was using foolish, silly talk with His Name.

For example, one night our son came over right at dinner time. I had a nice meal laid out on the table, and he just kept talking on and on about a lot of things I really didn't want to get into. When I saw that he was in no hurry to leave, I jokingly said to him, "Out, in the Name of Jesus!"

The moment I did that, heavy conviction fell on me because the Lord had been teaching me in that very area. I hear people say a lot of things like that in jest, but we need to be careful not to make jokes with the Name.

I once went to lunch with a powerful Christian intercessor who shares the Word on a regular basis. Five times in one hour I heard her take the Name of the Lord in vain (lightly and foolishly). Many times believers do that without realizing what they are doing.

When you use the Name of the Lord, make sure you are sincere. If you make a mistake because of bad habits, if you hear yourself slip and use the Name in an improper way, stop immediately and repent. Ask the Lord to forgive you for taking His Name in vain, but realize that you are actually hurting yourself when you use the Lord's Name in an improper way. If you expect the Name to release power in your life when you need it to, then you have to reverence the Name the rest of the time.

Power is immediately made available to us who believe when we speak the Name — power to use against the devil and all his hosts, power to help ourselves and power to bless others. I'm not talking about a dribble of power, but a mighty outpouring that can cause the blessings of God to chase us down in the street and overtake us!

A master key to that power is to speak that glorious Name — Jesus! — with reverence and respect.

5

REVERENCE
AND RESPECT
FOR THE NAME

. . . I am a great King, says the Lord of hosts,
and My name is terrible and to be [reverently]
feared among the nations.

Malachi 1:14

By the time you have reached this point
in the book, I hope you have come to
realize that the Name of Jesus is more
than just an ordinary Name. There is
power in the Name, and in this verse the
Lord Himself warns us that His Name is
to be reverently feared.

The word "fear" here means to show reverent trust, love and obedience toward Him.[1] In Proverbs 1:7 we are told, *The reverent and worshipful fear of the Lord is the beginning and the principal and choice part of knowledge . . . and godly Wisdom. . . .*

If you want to know the truth, I think many Christians today have lost a lot of reverence for many spiritual things.

When we learn that God is our Friend, we come into a much more comfortable relationship with Him. But some time ago He spoke to my heart that we need to be careful about getting Him on the "buddy system" so that we think of Him as just our "buddy" without realizing how great and awesome He is.

Reverence Provokes Obedience

Children, obey your parents in the Lord [as His representatives], for this is just and right.

Honor (esteem and value as precious) your father and your mother — this is the first commandment with a promise.

Ephesians 6:1,2

I believe if we were more reverent, we would be more obedient because reverence provokes obedience.

When children have reverence and respect for their parents, they don't argue with them or rebel against them.

I believe the reason many children don't respect and revere their parents as they should is that their parents have lost respect and reverence for spiritual things, spiritual leaders and authority figures in general. As a result, the lack of respect and reverence is passed down from parents to children so that they talk back, argue and rebel. If a parent openly displays disrespect toward their employer, they are teaching their children to be disrespectful also.

It is not at all uncommon these days to be in a public place like a store and see a two-year-old having a temper tantrum and actually hitting or kicking his mother. If we are not careful, that is the way our children will end up acting toward us and our heavenly Father. In other words, they will lose reverence and respect for us and for the Lord, as well as for all others in authority.

We must understand that this is what Satan tries to do. He causes things like disrespect and irreverence in the world, hoping they will creep their way into the church, because he knows that when they do, we become disobedient. Disobedience causes us to lose the power of God in our life.

One thing we must guard against to keep that from happening is familiarity.

Familiarity Breeds a Lack of Reverence

And when they came to Nacon's threshing floor, Uzzah put out his hand to the ark of God and took hold of it, for the oxen stumbled and shook it.

And the anger of the Lord was kindled against Uzzah; and God smote him there for touching the ark, and he died there by the ark of God.

2 Samuel 6:6,7

In this passage from the Old Testament, we see that David and his men were bringing the ark of the covenant back to Bethlehem. As they approached a certain place, the oxen that were pulling the cart with the ark in it stumbled, and the ark began to shake. Uzzah, a young man who was driving the cart, reached out to steady the ark . . . *and God struck him down there for his irreverence . . .* (v. 7 NASB), and he died instantly. (We read in Numbers chapters 3 and 4 that the Lord had given Moses specific directions about who could handle the ark and how it was to be transported.)

Verse 8 goes on to say that David was grieved and offended by Uzzah's death. He didn't understand why Uzzah had to die just for reaching out and touching the ark.

Earlier, in 1 Samuel 7, we read that when the ark was first returned to Israel by the Philistines, it was kept at the home of Abinadab, Uzzah's father, possibly for a number of years.

I believe it was because the ark had sat in his home for so long that it had become a commonplace thing to Uzzah so that he did not regard it with esteem. That's why he was not afraid to reach out and touch it — familiarity with the ark had bred a lack of reverence for it in him, and it cost him his life.[2]

Familiarity Limits Power

But Jesus said to them, A prophet is not without honor (deference, reverence) except in his [own] country and among [his] relatives and in his [own] house.

And He was not able to do even one work of power there, except that He laid His hands on a few sickly people [and] cured them.

And He marveled because of their unbelief. . . .

Mark 6:4-6

We have to be very careful about becoming overly familiar with things. Once we become too familiar with them, then we no longer show the respect for them that needs to be shown.

That is also true of familiarity with people.

I know that many people don't understand why spiritual leaders cannot always become "buddy-buddy," so to speak, with those to whom they minister. Many times if people come to know their spiritual leaders too well, they no longer see them in the position they need to be in to provide the help that is needed. It is human nature to begin to devaluate things that are too readily available.

In this passage in Mark 6, Jesus had gone to His hometown of Nazareth. When He began to preach in the synagogue there, many people were offended at Him. They recognized Him as the son of Mary. They knew His brothers and sisters. Their familiarity with Him caused them to be irreverent and disrespectful toward Him. As a result, His power to help them was limited, and He healed only a few sick people.

Sometimes a pastor can pray and pray for someone in his congregation without that person ever getting a breakthrough. Then a visiting evangelist can come into the church and pray for that individual, and he is healed immediately.

Why is that? Is the evangelist more anointed or more powerful than the pastor?

No, the reason is that the sick person sees the evangelist in a different way from the way he sees his pastor. He sees his pastor every week, so he becomes "good old Pastor Joe." Everyone loves him and thinks he is a great guy, but they don't put the faith in him that they put in someone they don't know.

Maybe the reason is that they have seen their pastor be human once in a while. Maybe they have seen him yell at his kids or be a little grouchy. So all of a sudden they can't handle the fact that he is a "regular person" just like themselves.

But what the people don't see is that the evangelist did similar kinds of things before he came to their church to minister!

Familiarity Lessens Respect

Is not this the Carpenter, the son of Mary and the brother of James and Joses and Judas and Simon? Are not His sisters here among us?

*And they took offense at Him and were hurt [that is, they disapproved of Him, and **it hindered them from acknowledging His authority**]....*

Mark 6:3

Sometimes when a person gets saved and receives a call of God upon his life, his family members and relatives cannot accept that call.

Do you know why? The reason is that they are too familiar with him. They know him too well to give him the respect they should.

As we have seen in this passage, that can happen to anyone, even Jesus. The Bible says that even His own brothers did not believe in Him. (John 7:5.)

I still have relatives who cannot receive my ministry the way other people do. Some of them have even told me, "You may be a hotshot now, but I knew you when. . . ."

Often some people won't let us get over our past. But the Bible says that if anyone is in Christ, he is a new creature; old things have passed away, and all things have become new. (2 Corinthians 5:17 KJV.)

We don't want to become so familiar with the Name of Jesus that we just throw it around thoughtlessly without any understanding that there is more to it than speaking the Name.

I don't know about you, but when I speak the Name, "Jesus," I can actually **feel** the anointing that is upon it. When I speak it in my meetings, people get saved, healed and filled with the Holy Spirit.

Those kinds of results are not limited to people in ministry. That is why I have a deep desire for every believer to understand about having reverence and respect for that glorious Name. When we do, we open ourselves up to the power in the Name — power to handle our own circumstances and to minister supernaturally to others.

6
THE NAME
AND RELATIONSHIP

~

And after He had appeared in human form, He abased and humbled Himself [still further] and carried His obedience to the extreme of death, even the death of the cross!

Therefore [because He stooped so low] God has highly exalted Him and has freely bestowed on Him the name that is above every name,

That in (at) the name of Jesus every knee should (must) bow, in heaven and on earth and under the earth,

~

*And every tongue [frankly and openly] confess
and acknowledge that Jesus Christ is Lord, to
the glory of God the Father.*

Philippians 2:8-11

How did Jesus get the Name we've been talking about which is so powerfully described in this passage, a Name which is synonymous with such names as Lord, Savior, the Word (John 1:1), Lamb of God (John 1:29), Bread of Life (John 6:35), Lord of lords and King of kings (Revelation 17:14)?

He got it by being extremely **obedient.**

We have already discussed obedience, but there is another aspect of it in connection with the Name that I want to touch on next.

Obedience and Relationship

*Let this same attitude and purpose and
[humble] mind be in you which was in Christ
Jesus: [Let Him be your example in humility:]*

*Who, although **being essentially one with
God** and in the form of God [possessing the
fullness of the attributes which make God
God], did not think this equality with God
was a thing to be eagerly grasped or retained,*

*But stripped Himself [of all privileges and
rightful dignity], so as to assume the guise of a
servant (slave), in that He became like men
and was born a human being.*

Philippians 2:5-7

In this passage we see that before Jesus'
act of obedience (described in Philippians
2:8-11 at the beginning of this chapter),

He had a pre-existing and ongoing relationship with the Father.

If using the Name of Jesus is going to produce powerful results in our life, we must first have a relationship with Him, just as He had with the Father in heaven.

Having a relationship with someone comes from spending time with that person. To have a close relationship with the Lord we must have a regular time that we spend with Him in fellowship. That simply means talking to Him daily, reading His Word regularly and letting Him get involved in our life.

It is not possible to have a true relationship with Him without commitment — the same kind of commitment that is made in a marriage.

To Use the Name,
We Must Be Married!

He who has the bride is the bridegroom. . . .

John 3:29

In the Bible, Jesus presented Himself as a bridegroom and the church as His bride. In order to have a bridegroom and a bride, there must be a wedding, a marriage. That marriage produces a lasting personal relationship between the bride and groom.

When Dave Meyer and I were married, I took his name. I became Mrs. Dave Meyer. Now I have all the authority that the name "Dave Meyer" represents.

Before we were married, I didn't have anything. He had a new car. The minute we became husband and wife, that car became mine.

Before we were married, I had debts. The minute we were married, those debts became Dave's.

All that we had individually became ours corporately because we were in marital relationship one with the other.

That was not the case when we were just dating. I did not get the name "Dave Meyer" or anything that name represents until we were married.

That is the way it is with Jesus; we don't get His Name and all the power it confers until we are "married" to Him.

The problem is that too many Christians just want to "date" Jesus. They want to live their own lives their own way, independently. They don't want to give Him their all. They want to withhold some areas of their life. They don't want to make a complete commitment.

Yet when they get into trouble or they have a disaster, it's:

Oh, Jesus, I'm in trouble! Let's have a date!

Oh, Jesus, I need some money! Let's have a date!

Oh, Jesus, I'm sick! Let's have a date!

They want to be able to call upon that Name to provide the money or healing or deliverance or whatever they need. But they don't want to belong to Him totally and all the time.

Jesus is not interested in just having a "date" with us occasionally. He wants a permanent relationship with us. He wants to put a ring of relationship on our finger and "marry" us. He wants us to receive Him as our "Husband," as our one and only Lord and Master. (See Isaiah 54:5.)

The trouble is, too often we are not willing to make that kind of commitment. We want to use the Name, but we must realize that **we don't get to use the Name until we get married.**

I didn't get to use the name of my husband until I married him. As long as we were just dating, I couldn't sign his name and get money out of his bank account. But the moment we were married, I could draw upon everything he had in the bank because whatever he had was mine — and vice versa.

Jesus told me a long time ago (not audibly, but in my heart), "If you give Me everything you have, I will give you everything I have. Everything that is Mine will be at your disposal. But you have to belong to Me."

In other words, He wants us to turn all of our attention toward Him, to go after Him full force, to give Him our all.

Why?

His power comes only from relationship with Him, from belonging to Him.

Belonging Brings Power

But as many as did receive and welcome Him,
He gave the authority (power, privilege, right)
to become the children of God, that is, to those

*who believe in (adhere to, trust in, and rely
on) His name.*

John 1:12

I have a sense in my life, and it grows all
the time, that I belong to God.

What do I mean?

I am not my own. I can't just go
through life doing what I want to do,
acting any way I want to, spending
money on anything I want to, treating
people any way I want to.

God allows me to do a lot of things I
want to do. I don't go around asking
Him if every little thing I do all day long
is His will before I do it.

I believe we are led by the Holy Spirit in
the routine affairs of everyday life, as
well as the out-of-the-ordinary matters

114

that arise occasionally. But the moment I get a signal from God that something I am about to do is wrong, I stop myself immediately.

Why do I do that? Because I have a reverential fear of losing the Presence of God.

Yes, I am afraid, but afraid in the right way. I am not afraid of God, but I am afraid of getting up in front of thousands of people who are waiting for me to bring them the Word and power of the Lord — and having nothing happen because I have lost God's Presence and anointing in my life!

That is scary. And it should be. It keeps me in prayer and obedience. It keeps me turning the television off when I hear the Name of the Lord being taken in vain.

I have made a commitment to the Lord. I belong to Him, and as a result, I have experienced His power time after time when I pray in His Name.

It is amazing how many Christians never make a commitment to the Lord and never experience His power in their life. They are saved, and they will go to heaven some day when they die. But they are living a powerless life on this earth.

They do not understand that belonging brings power.

I realize that one reason they do not make a commitment is that the word "commitment" makes them uncomfortable. They think they will have to give up something. Really, they will gain every-thing. (See Matthew 19:29 TLB.)

Do not think that the Lord expects you to be perfect. When you belong to Him, you can trust Him to help you keep your commitment to Him.

Just do what you can do, and He will help you do what you cannot do.

Making a commitment to the Lord is actually a two-way covenant. We commit our all to Him, and He has committed to be with us always. (See Matthew 28:20.)

How is He with us?

Never forget that He is with us in His Name. Every single, solitary time we speak it, He is there with us to help us when we need help and to empower us to accomplish all He has planned for our life.

There is power in the wonderful Name of Jesus. He desires to use that power to help us, heal us and radically and outrageously bless us.

I pray that you will make a vow that from this moment on, you are going to live each day committed to Him and go forth in the power of Jesus' Name — **the Name above all names!**

CONCLUSION

. . . By what sort of power or by what kind of authority did [such people as] you do this [healing]?

Then Peter . . . said to them. . . . Let it be known and understood by all of you . . . that in the name and through the power and authority of Jesus Christ of Nazareth . . . this man is standing here before you well and sound in body.

Acts 4:7,8,10

Enough cannot be said about the power of the Name of Jesus. His Name is more powerful than anything else in heaven and earth — and we as believers have been given the right to use that Name for any situation in life.

I don't think there is anything sadder than to see a child of God praying and doing other things that Christians do, but not having any power in his life to get results.

The weaknesses the world has are not our inheritance.

Jesus did not come to earth, die on the cross and rise again on the third day for us to be weak and defeated. He went through all that to give us an inheritance — authority in this life and power to rule over our circumstances through His Name.

In this book, I have shared keys to receiving that power which the Lord has shown me. Remember, you receive His power through faith in the Name of Jesus, through praying in faith in His Name, through reverence and respect for His Name and through relationship with Him.

I believe good things are going to happen to you as you begin applying these principles in your life.

There is power available to you to meet every need. As you learn to exercise your right to use the Name of Jesus against those needs, you will see them change through the power of Jesus' Name — **the Name above all names.**

Prayer for a Personal Relationship with the Lord

God wants you to receive His free gift of salvation. Jesus wants to save you and fill you with the Holy Spirit more than anything. If you have never invited Jesus, the Prince of Peace, to be your Lord and Savior, I invite you to do so now. Pray the following prayer, and if you are really sincere about it, you will experience a new life in Christ.

Father,

You loved the world so much, You gave Your only begotten Son to die for our sins so that whoever believes in Him will not perish, but have eternal life.

Your Word says we are saved by grace through faith as a gift from You. There is nothing we can do to earn salvation.

I believe and confess with my mouth that Jesus Christ is Your Son, the Savior of the world. I believe He died on the cross for me and bore all of my sins, paying the price for them. I believe in my heart that You raised Jesus from the dead.

I ask You to forgive my sins. I confess Jesus as my Lord. According to Your Word, I am saved and will spend eternity with You! Thank You, Father. I am so grateful! In Jesus' Name, amen.

See John 3:16; Ephesians 2:8,9; Romans 10:9,10; 1 Corinthians 15:3,4; 1 John 1:9; 4:14-16; 5:1,12,13.

ENDNOTES

Chapter 2

[1] Believers ". . . are led by the Spirit of God, as a scholar in his learning is led by his tutor, as a traveler in his journey is led by his guide, as a soldier in his engagements is led by his captain; not driven as beasts, but led as rational creatures, drawn with the cords of a man and the bands of love. . . . Having submitted themselves in believing to his guidance, they do in their obedience follow that guidance and are sweetly led into all truth and all duty." *MATTHEW HENRY'S COMMENTARY ON THE WHOLE BIBLE,* New Modern Edition Electronic Database, copyright © 1991 by Hendrickson Publishers, Inc., s.v. "Romans 8:10-16, The believer's privilege." Used by permission. All rights reserved.

[2] *American Dictionary of the English Language,* 10th Ed. (San Francisco: Foundation for

American Christian Education, 1998). Facsimile of Noah Webster's 1828 edition, permission to reprint by G. & C. Merriam Company, copyright © 1967 & 1995 (Renewal) by Rosalie J. Slater, s.v. "ABIDE."

Chapter 3

1 The Bible teaches that we can have complete forgiveness of our sins (total freedom from condemnation) through the blood of Jesus. The circulation of our blood through our body is actually a continual "washing" or cleansing process that "washes" our system from waste material that would otherwise poison it. In the same way, when we confess our sins to God, the blood of Jesus (which He shed when He died on the cross for our sins) continually "washes" our inner man from sin that poisons us spiritually. (See 1 John 1:7, 9 TLB).

2 Matthew 9:5 TLB tells us, *I* (Jesus) . . . *have the authority on earth to forgive sins.*

Chapter 4

[1] William Smith, LL.D., *Smith's Bible Dictionary* (Old Tappan, New Jersey: Spire Books, Jove Publications, Inc., for the Fleming H. Revell Company, 1981), p. 213, s.v. "GOD."

Chapter 5

[1] *Jamieson, Fausset and Brown Commentary,* Electronic Database, copyright © 1997 by Biblesoft, s.v. "fear." All rights reserved,

[2] "Uzzah's offence seems very small. He and his brother Ahio, the sons of Abinadab, in whose house the ark had long been lodged, having been used to attend it. . .undertook to drive the cart in which the ark was carried. . . . By some accident or other the ark was in danger of being overthrown. Uzzah thereupon laid hold of it, to save it from falling, we have reason to think with a very good intention, to preserve the reputation of the ark and to prevent a bad omen. Yet this was his crime. Uzzah was a Levite, but priests

only might touch the ark. The law was express concerning the Kohathites, that, though they were to carry the ark by the staves, yet they must not touch any holy thing, lest they die. (Numbers 4:15.) Uzzah's long familiarity with the ark, and the constant attendance he had given to it, might occasion his presumption, but would not excuse it." *MATTHEW HENRY'S COMMENTARY ON THE WHOLE BIBLE*, s.v. 2 Samuel 6:6-11, "Uzzah slain for touching the ark."

About the Author

Joyce Meyer has been teaching the Word of God since 1976 and in full-time ministry since 1980. She is the bestselling author of more than sixty inspirational books, including *In Pursuit of Peace, How to Hear from God, Knowing God Intimately*, and *Battlefield of the Mind*. She has also released thousands of teaching cassettes and a complete video library. Joyce's *Enjoying Everyday Life* radio and television programs are broadcast around the world, and she travels extensively conducting conferences. Joyce and her husband, Dave, are the parents of four grown children and make their home in St. Louis, Missouri.

To contact the author write:

Joyce Meyer Ministries
P.O. Box 655
Fenton, Missouri 63026
or call: (636) 349-0303
Internet Address: www.joycemeyer.org

*Please include your testimony or help
received from this book when you write.
Your prayer requests are welcome.*

To contact the author
in Canada, please write:
Joyce Meyer Ministries Canada, Inc.
Lambeth Box 1300
London, ON N6P 1T5
or call: (636) 349-0303

In Australia, please write:
Joyce Meyer Ministries-Australia
Locked Bag 77
Mansfield Delivery Centre
Queensland 4122
or call: (07) 3349 1200

In England, please write:
Joyce Meyer Ministries
P.O. Box 1549
Windsor
SL4 1GT
or call: 01753 831102

Books by Joyce Meyer

Battlefield of the Kid's Mind (Spring 2006)
Approval Addiction (Spring 2005)
Ending Your Day Right
In Pursuit of Peace
The Secret Power of Speaking God's Word
Seven Things That Steal Your Joy
Starting Your Day Right
Beauty for Ashes Revised Edition
How to Hear from God
How to Hear from God Study Guide
Knowing God Intimately
The Power of Forgiveness
The Power of Determination
The Power of Being Positive
The Secrets of Spiritual Power
The Battle Belongs to the Lord
Secrets to Exceptional Living
Eight Ways to Keep the Devil Under Your Feet
Teenagers Are People Too!
Filled with the Spirit
Celebration of Simplicity
The Joy of Believing Prayer
Never Lose Heart
Being the Person God Made You to Be

A Leader in the Making
"Good Morning, This Is God!" Gift Book
Jesus—Name Above All Names
"Good Morning, This Is God!" Daily Calendar
Making Marriage Work
(Previously published as *Help Me—I'm Married!*)
Reduce Me to Love
Be Healed in Jesus' Name
How to Succeed at Being Yourself
Eat and Stay Thin
Weary Warriors, Fainting Saints
Life in the Word Journal
Life in the Word Devotional
Be Anxious for Nothing
Be Anxious for Nothing Study Guide
Straight Talk Omnibus
Straight Talk on Loneliness
Straight Talk on Fear
Straight Talk on Insecurity
Straight Talk on Discouragement
Straight Talk on Worry
Straight Talk on Depression
Straight Talk on Stress
Don't Dread
Managing Your Emotions
Healing the Brokenhearted

Me and My Big Mouth!
Me and My Big Mouth! Study Guide
Prepare to Prosper
Do It Afraid!
Expect a Move of God in Your Life…Suddenly!
Enjoying Where You Are on the Way to
Where You Are Going
The Most Important Decision You Will Ever Make
When, God, When?
Why, God, Why?
The Word, the Name, the Blood
Battlefield of the Mind
Battlefield of the Mind Study Guide
Tell Them I Love Them
Peace
The Root of Rejection
If Not for the Grace of God
If Not for the Grace of God Study Guide

JOYCE MEYER SPANISH TITLES
Las Siete Cosas Que Te Roban el Gozo
(Seven Things That Steal Your Joy)
Empezando Tu Día Bien (Starting Your Day Right)

BY DAVE MEYER
Life Lines